PRAISE FOR *NO BETTER PLACE: A NEW ZEN PRIMER*

"While *No Better Place* may seem like a slight book, it's actually a wide-open doorway—into the essence of Zen! It says so much so succinctly and insightfully, that reading its brief chapters brings real "Aha!" delight. I look forward to sharing this book with my own Zen students. Many thanks to Hoag Holmgren!"

> —Rafe Martin Sensei, award-winning author,
> founding teacher and spiritual director,
> Endless Path Zendo

"Among the Zen handbooks or primers out there, none fit your hand so simply as these sixty-four poetry-like chapters of Hoag Holmgren's *No Better Place*. Like the sixty-four hexagrams of the *I Ching*, each widens into a far-off state of mind. Turn them over in your thoughts though, and they prove to be guides to where you are standing. Ten in particular, which refer to the 12th century Chinese Oxherding Pictures, point North American Zen back to a mythic world of ancestors. Old-time buddhas, those ancestors. They are our brothers and

sisters in the ecology of mind. Thanks to Holmgren's book, you can stand eyebrow-to-eyebrow with them."
—**Andrew Schelling, editor of** ***The Wisdom Anthology of North American Buddhist Poetry***

"No Better Place is simple, clear, and beautifully written. I highly recommend it for anyone (new or experienced) interested in the path of Zen. This book captures the heart of this journey and beckons one to step in."
—**Peggy Metta Sheehan, Sensei, Zen Center of Denver**

"*No Better Place* is a penetrating and affecting presentation of the Buddha Dharma cast in a thoroughly Western idiom. Hoag's simple, clear prose invites entry in this very place, now."
—**Danan Henry Roshi**

"Hoag Holmgren writes from the depths of his own understanding in this profound and simply expressed primer. These words will touch and inspire readers to surrender to a joyful experience of compassion for all."
—**Jiun Hosen, Osho, Abbess, Bodhi Manda Zen Center**

NO BETTER PLACE

A NEW ZEN PRIMER

Books may be purchased in quantity and/or special sales by contacting the publisher. All inquiries related to such matters should be addressed to:

Middle Creek Publishing & Audio
9027 Cascade Avenue
Beulah, CO 81023
editor@middlecreekpublishing.com
(719) 369-9050

First Paperback Edition, 2019
ISBN: 978-0-9989322-9-3

Printed in the United States

Cover Image & Design: Susan LeGrande |
https://susanlegrande.carbonmade.com/

Catherine Jao | *Ten Ox-herding Pictures* (2012) and *Enso* (2018)
Sumi ink on handmade paper mounted on shikishi
catherine.c.jao@gmail.com | www.facebook.com/catherine.jao.art

Author photo: Leda Swann

NO BETTER PLACE

A NEW ZEN PRIMER

HOAG HOLMGREN

Middle Creek Publishing & Audio
Beulah, CO
↑

ALSO BY HOAG HOLMGREN

p a l e o s

Meaningful Grading:
a Guide for Faculty in the Arts (co-author)

for my teacher Danan Henry Roshi

for the Old Bones Sangha

for the Zen Center of Denver Sangha

NINE BOWS

Open are the double doors of the horizon;
unlocked are its bolts.

Utterance 220, The Pyramid of Unas,
Egypt, 2345 BCE

I am he as you are he as you are me
and we are all together.

"I am the Walrus," The Beatles,
EMI Studios, London, 1967 CE

1

Zen Buddhism is a path of waking up to the vastness of who you are. To uncover this aspect of self-nature—usually hidden beneath layers of habitual thinking—is to be free from alienation, pettiness, and self-preoccupation. It is to live with greater clarity, creativity, joy, and kind-heartedness. But what is this expansiveness? If we look for an answer in the world's sacred texts, the list of descriptors is long and rather exotic-sounding: *birthless, deathless, unborn, divine, eternal, holy, unnamable, unknowable, unspeakable, unfathomable, adamantine*, and so on. Buddhist and Taoist terms include *Dharma, Supreme Source, Dharmakaya, Tao, Essence, Shunyata, Luminous Ground, Buddha Nature, Buddha Mind*, and *Universal Mind*. From the 20th century we have Paul Tillich's *ground of being* and Shunryu Suzuki's *universal being*. Alan Watts preferred *the which than which there is no whicher*. Zen teachers speak of *no-self, emptiness*, and *the dropping away of body and mind*. Unfortunately, such phrases and labels can sound forbidding and otherworldly as though who we are is somehow beyond our ability to realize. But this great unbrokenness can never be elsewhere. It's always right here, closer than each breath, unmoving in the midst of all arrivals and departures.

2

In the 19th century, Henry David Thoreau famously claimed that most people lead lives of quiet desperation. Given the extent of despair, unrest, and general unhappiness in the world today, such a sweeping assertion is likely still valid. Quiet desperation can be the nagging sense that something important is missing from your life. It can be the feeling of being psychologically tasered by the plight of the world. It can arise from knowing that you'll die some day but not knowing when, how, or where. And it can manifest as a slow-burning hunger for some shred of illumination regarding the mystery of this strange, ephemeral phenomenon of being alive now and embodied here. Whatever guise desperation may take, the practice of Zen is a kind of antidote. It is a way to pause and let the fortifying depths find you. It is a delicious unraveling of the antiquated belief that you're just some sliver of meat, isolated and adrift in an infinite cosmos.

3

Zazen—silent, seated meditation—is the internal combustion engine of Zen practice. But zazen is not merely transportive. It is itself the abandonment of philosophy and the reclamation of existential wealth. What's reclaimed? Just this: there is nothing to be reclaimed. The life you're living is already inviolable. The vital organs of your body can't be counted because they include the shadows of clouds crossing the valley, snowflakes disappearing into surf, the old dog barking next door.

4

When we focus wholeheartedly on the breath, our hyperloops of thinking lose solidity and speed. We gain a little perspective and learn to see how we dwell within a moat of mentation. And this dwelling can be "an imprisonment so total that the prisoner doesn't even know he's locked up," in the words of David Foster Wallace. But when the mind becomes quiet, a lost continent emerges from the fog. To encounter this groundless ground is to find, despite cultural programming, that we're not obstructed by anything. We're not lacking anything. All quadrants and all dimensions of time and space are collaborating in this moment as this moment. There is no thing and no one outside, apart, or alien. There are no strangers, as Thomas Merton put it.

5

The zazen posture, whether on a cushion or in a chair, is a straight back, an alert forward-facing head, eyes half open and softly focused, the gaze lowered. The lower back gently and naturally curves in. Breathing is comfortably anchored in the belly. The left hand rests on the right hand, palms up, thumb tips touching lightly to make a soft circle or oval. The mind's allegiance shifts to the breath, to the awareness of bodily sensations, to the immediacy of what's actually occurring right now, here. In this way, zazen is a voyage. There is no departure and no arrival but belief, faith, and views are left behind. It's a journey of verifying via direct experience what the Buddha verified: that you and all rivers, mountains, spiral galaxies, and beings have the same last name.

6

When our natural spaciousness begins to function in daily life, we can relate to the world and to others a little more sanely. We're less frequently held hostage by moldering narratives and merry-go-rounds of thinking. Life becomes less tightly spooled. We see that we can live quite well without the yoke of private manifestos, agendas, and expectations. It's enough to show up with empty hands. It's enough to do what we're doing. Making hot chocolate, changing a diaper, flipping a pancake. Each moment possesses depth and completeness. And when you see that the other is also not other, you begin to see with the eyes of a Buddha which are precisely the ordinary, precious eyes you've always had.

7

The discipline of seated stillness is older than we'll ever know. It pre-dates the historical Buddha and may have been discovered as far back as the Upper Paleolithic when aspects of hunting and survival surely depended upon periodically being still and silent. These days we feel little need to be still and silent. We like perpetual motion, perpetual busy-ness, and perpetual stimulation. Our lives are thus perpetually unsettled. The body is the material wing of the mind, and the mind is the immaterial wing of the body. What we do to one we do to the other. This is why being physically still is an essential element of zazen. It can seem counterintuitive, but if the body leads, the mind follows.

8

Despite the ubiquity of dazzling technology, there has been no measurable decline in rates of mass depression, loneliness, or anxiety. On the contrary, we're more stressed out and medicated than ever. Each software upgrade and advance in technology seems to promise another step toward omnipotence and omniscience but it never quite delivers. Zen practice swims against the riptide of 24/7 infotainment and our tendency to sleepwalk through entire neighborhoods of our life. We become reacquainted with something elemental and nourishing, something already here. In the early years of practice it's like discovering a new room in your home. It has always been there but you've never noticed. The windows are open, the sun is burning, and the songs of the birds have no problem mingling with the sounds of traffic.

9

Zen Buddhism is similar to other disciplines and traditions in that it's crucial at some point to train with a teacher. A teacher keeps our practice alive and vital. He or she meets with students privately (dokusan); gives periodic Dharma talks (teishō); and there is ongoing interaction in meetings, social gatherings, and communal work periods. She gives, she takes away, she supports, she thwarts. A teacher senses when we should transition to a new practice: from breath-counting to following the breath, for example. He knows when we have grasped the essential nugget of a koan, and sees when we're lost in a suckhole of self-preoccupation. When the time is right, the teacher might introduce the subtle non-practice of shikantaza (just sitting), and of course supports our practice off the cushion, in the world. In short, a teacher helps fulfill Ruth Fuller Sasaki's vision of the three essentials of Zen training: zazen, the study of koans, and daily life. Without a teacher's guidance, we can easily drift into a subtle purgatory where "Zen practice tends to become a hobby, made to fit the needs of the ego," as Robert Aitken put it.

10

"The solution to the problem of life is seen in the vanishing of this problem," says Ludwig Wittgenstein. Indeed, there are no tidy solutions to the big questions. But when there is no highway of thinking cutting you off from the world, there is also no paradox about life and death. There is just intimacy. In the deep-water stillness of zazen, this means that there is just breathing. The breath devours you. You don't know if you're breathing the breath or if the breath is breathing you. Off the meditation cushion this means that there is only the lone coyote trotting across the dirt road. There is no detached observer categorizing and labeling. There's just taking care of a sick child. Just mourning the loss of a loved one. Just watering the garden and pulling weeds. Just this hook of moon rising above treeline, closer than your hand.

11

To speak of the Dharma as though it were untethered from the phenomenal world of meteor showers and seagulls only perpetuates and strengthens the fiction of this versus that. This is why Zen teachers prefer to talk about ordinary subjects such as meteor showers and seagulls. There is no need for hushed voices or secret handshakes. There is no cloud of uncut Dharma floating around in some other dimension. William Blake was right about holding "...infinity in the palm of your hand / And eternity in an hour." Every drop of the Dharmic ocean is included in the act of throwing a tennis ball for your dog. It's not much of a Dharma if it's more accessible in the next life or in some other country or if it only reveals itself to certain people speaking certain languages. Zen practice allows us to step past concepts and experience the Buddha Dharma as nothing other than this one perfectly imperfect life. Can you encounter the Buddha in a broken pine needle? If not there, where?

12

"All the way to heaven is heaven," said Saint Catherine of Siena. There is no there to get to. Each step treads on it. Each step is it. There is no place or dimension in the cosmos more cosmic than where you are right now. There is no being in the cosmos more cosmic than you.

13

The universe is not trying to tell you something or send you a message. The universe is not trying to teach you a lesson. This is because you and the universe cannot be pulled apart. This is what Master Wu-Men realized when he said, "My body's so big there's no place to put it." This is what Pema Chödrön realized when she said, "You're always in the middle of a sacred circle." This is what Yasutani Roshi realized when he said, "When you hear about no-self, don't be sad. Thanks to no-self, the entire universe is self." This is what Eihei Dōgen realized when he said, "Mind is no other than mountains and rivers and the great wide Earth, the sun and the moon and the stars." This original identity is what sincere and engaged practitioners, monastic and lay, have realized over the centuries and continue to realize today.

14

It can be inspiring to hear scientists describe the universe in ways that accord with Buddhist teachings: *The universe is permeated by a seamless field of energy (Higgs Field). Biology is constructed from the detritus of exploded stars. Space and time are inseparable.* But this is ultimately just data that gets filed away with other data. Again quoting Wittgenstein, "Even if all possible scientific questions be answered, the problems of life have still not been touched at all." Scientific answers, as useful as they are in expanding our knowledge of the world, tend to have little transformative power on a personal scale. For example, a thorough understanding of quantum gravity probably won't deepen our patience, make us better listeners, increase our generosity, amplify our creativity, mitigate the fear of death, or enhance our parenting skills. Thus the power of slow-cooking in the kiln of zazen. In the kiln of zazen, we get out of the way and learn to live the problems of life more authentically. Concern for the opinions of others, scheming, evasion, self-aggrandizement, self-disparagement, and certainty burn away. What remains? If you say "nothing" you miss it. If you remain silent you miss it. If you say something like "everything," "awareness," "love," or "pure being" you also miss it.

15

The smell of rain walking in through the front door doesn't need anything. Tuesday's overcast sky isn't a bad omen. Yet how easy it is to miss the perfection of things as they are. When we're stuck in what Antonin Artaud calls the "narrow chambers of the brain," the castles of me, my, and mine dominate the skyline. In such a space, the beauty and wonder of the world fade to a kind of background noise. We can comment on the aesthetics of snow but we remain a detached onlooker. How much more expansive and gratifying it is to dwell in the shire of not-knowing. In the shire of not-knowing, there is no quarantined I seeing snow for the thousandth time. There is just snow, just cold air, just this bare aspen tree seen for the *only* time—without the labels of snow, cold air, tree. This is the world prior to classification. When we're not blinded by the grids we superimpose on the world, every being, place, and thing reveals itself as some kind of wordless miracle. The fallacy of the mundane is laid bare. Walt Whitman seemed to know something about all this when he wrote:

> WHY! who makes much of a miracle?
> As to me, I know of nothing else but miracles

16

The shire of not-knowing is simply the hour shorn of categories, labels, and descriptions. It has nothing to do with ignorance and everything to do with no separation. Where there is no separation, there is no you being mindful of a singing chickadee. In the shire of not-knowing, <your name here> is replaced by birdsong.

17

Knowing is an essential part of being human but it also tends to hog the camera and obscure the unutterable. When we know something, or profess to knowing it, we are dead to it being anything else. If we can't remove this straightjacket of certainty, life feels already lived and we're just X-ing off the days with a Sharpie. The shire of not-knowing is the mind of the jazz guitarist not having a clue what note she will play next. It's the mind of the novelist blind to how the story will end but utterly absorbed in writing. It's the mind of a parent reaching out to catch a teetering toddler at the top of the stairs. No hidden motive, no mire of deliberation. When there's no subject-object duality of knower and known, the act of chopping cilantro becomes our true home.

18

The path of Zen is demanding and challenging, but it's not complicated. When lost in the boulevards and back alleys of mind, we're estranged from the world and from each other. When intimate with each act and each moment, we're reunited with a place beyond knowing and ignorance. Just don't think that this place can be located with GPS. Nor is *place* a metaphor for some higher, or better, dimension.

A monk once asked Hsūan-sha, "How can I enter the Tao?"

Hsūan-sha replied, "Do you hear the sound of that stream?"

The monk said, "Yes."

"Enter there," said Hsūan-sha.

The head monk stood up and asked, "What if there's no stream?" he asked.

"Enter *there*," said Hsūan-sha.

19

I t's easy to see how a hanging tapestry is an amalgam of stitched together panels and threads. Yet we have a hard time seeing how thoroughly interwoven all things are everywhere. It's not that everything is connected; we are in fact inseparable from the blue jay, the Douglas Fir, the dirt road, the homeless person, the limousine, the horizon. This is the original face, the seamless roil of birth and death which is itself indestructible and ungraspable. When we're intimate with this boundlessness, our neighbor's joy is our joy; our friend's pain is our pain. Like the Grinch whose "small heart grew three sizes that day," we find that we possess the superpower of compassion. Compassion is the great love for all beings that spontaneously arises when we see that the world, in the words of Ta-man Hung-jen, "never divides itself into self and other, or subject and object, but merely wears the face of self and other."

20

Superpowers like compassion are the ways in which Zen practice functions in the world. They are not the ordinary worldly powers of controlling others, getting what you want, or doing whatever you want whenever you want. They are nonetheless true superpowers because they spring from selflessness. Another super-power is the ability to be unhindered by circumstances, whether it's being stuck in rush hour traffic, shopping at Costco, or dying. It is, as Robert Aitken put it, being at ease whether in comfort or discomfort. When Shunryu Suzuki was dying from stomach cancer he, not surprisingly, experienced profound pain and discomfort. One of his students was visibly shaken by this, thinking that a great Zen master should not die in so ignoble a manner. Suzuki Roshi said to him, "If you see me suffering, that's OK. That's just suffering Buddha." To be free in your current situation is to be one with that situation. If you die painlessly, that's fine. If you die in pain, that can also be fine. Easy to say, not so easy to do.

But if we can cooperate with the internal weather in a deep way, we find that there's no problem being grumpy Buddha, happy Buddha, stressed Buddha, horny Buddha, or tired Buddha. Each Buddha is perfectly just that Buddha. Each Buddha is capable of revising the essay, renovating the kitchen, volunteering at the homeless shelter, or launching the new business. No need to wait for a better, shinier Buddha. But how to manage all these Buddhas? Indeed, how many Buddhas are there? Hint: the answer is not a number.

21

Another superpower is the ability to serve others and work without burnout, resentment, self con-gratulation, or pride. This means doing what needs to be done moment to moment with no resistance. Cleaning the toilet is not inferior to surfing Hawaii's North Shore. If an act inhabits us completely, there's no room or need for comparing it with another act. Each act is just each act. But this requires a real generosity of the heart. Like a tree that offers shade equally to popes and peasants, it's possible to serve others without the baggage of self-conscious intent. Yet it's not about being a pushover or a doormat. Sometimes the appropriately generous act is a stern riposte, the withholding of money, or having your teenager take out the garbage.

22

The stability of the zazen posture declares *it's all here*. Each place is both center and circumference. Each place includes all places so there is always only *here*. There is no place more holy than where you are standing. Zazen reveals each person, thing, and moment to be the Tao and the Tao to be each person, thing, and moment. If we can genuinely grok this, we unlock the superpower of saving the world wherever we are by listening sincerely to an annoying co-worker; anonymously doing a good deed for a stranger; or playing with our children without watching the clock.

23

There's a story about the Zen teacher Philip Kapleau which illustrates the superpower of invisibility. He was alone at the Rochester Zen Center in the 1970s when a woman stopped by for a visit after reading his best-selling book *The Three Pillars of Zen*. He spoke with the woman for a while and answered her many questions, some of which were about his book. As she left, he gave her materials about the next introductory seminar. When the woman returned to attend the seminar, she was startled to see that the man who had spoken to her a few weeks prior was Philip Kapleau. He hadn't referred to himself as a teacher, and never self-identified as the author of the book she was raving about. He had simply talked to her and answered her questions. The woman admitted that at the time she had assumed he was a friendly janitor or groundskeeper. When Kapleau Roshi heard about this he was delighted and said that such a misunderstanding was the highest honor any Zen practitioner could receive. Zen is not about presenting oneself to others as a white-gloved sommelier of Buddhist esoterica. It's about becoming so natural and transparent that pretense and self promotion sit in the back seat and someone else's needs come into focus.

24

Zazen is a gentle *coup d'état* of the linear, the logical, and the certain: those limited habits of mind that so often govern the days. But practice is not a matter of simply easing into a Jacuzzi of oceanic oneness. We must summon the courage to face and let go of fears, demons, regrets, boredom, fantasies, physical discomfort, and persnickety vines of thinking until we find the unhewn bedrock at the heart of it all. And then the challenge is to deepen and clarify this revelation and its many implications. Zen practice is challenging mostly because it works. The narrow, limited sense of self really does begin to drop away. The mind really does begin to settle. Samadhi, a subtle state of boundless, healing absorption, really does emerge and inform daily life. But we may not want a panoramic view of the coast after all. Freedom can be scary. We might prefer the familiarity of the old slot canyon where every inch is known and only a sliver of sky is visible. Half asleep, I stalk my little fiefdom—a Minotaur in his labyrinth—dreaming the well-worn dream of me. There's nothing bad or wrong with this but it's the main reason why we so readily abandon, suspend, or postpone the rigors of any demanding practice (whether Zen, poetry, or physics). We may like the idea of diving into the unknown but we're often unwilling to truly leave the map behind.

25

In order to venture past the initial stage of settling the mind, there must be an urgency to liberate oneself from the Gordian knot of me, my, and mine: the root cause of human suffering. There must be an intuition that there *is* something profound to be uncovered in this life—something beyond the limited, finite self—and that even if we live a long life there's not much time. The path may begin with one of the great questions. Why is there so much suffering in the world? Who am I? What's the point of existence? What am I doing here? Or maybe we feel like we're dangling above some terrifying void— suspended in mid-air between womb and tomb—and simply yearn for a little peace of mind. Or perhaps like a pre-Socratic philosopher, we hunger to unlock the mysteries of the physical world. Whatever the case, the dis-ease of internal turmoil must be greater than any discomfort encountered while sitting still. The wish for resolution and insight must become an imperative, as unquestioned as eating and breathing. Whether or not the path is convenient, easy, or comfortable is irrelevant. Anaïs Nin famously put it this way: "And the day came when the risk to remain tight in a bud was more painful than the risk it took to blossom."

26

The main stages of Zen practice and realization are depicted in the *Ten Oxherding Pictures*, a 12th century Chinese collection of illustrations and poetry inspired by the *Maha Gopalaka Sutra*, a Pali text commonly translated as *The Greater Oxherd Discourse*. While each step along the path is the Tao itself, it's also the case that the path unfolds in phases that have unique characteristics. But these phases do not always progress in a linear fashion and we can't say that one is superior to another. And none are exhaustible or permanent. They are fluid in nature and more like stations of a mandala that the practitioner occupies at various times. In the first picture, *The Search for the Ox*, a solitary seeker—the Oxherder—is on a quest in a wild, thicket-ridden landscape. What's crucial here is that the search for the Ox has begun. The Ox symbolizes our birthless, deathless nature. Even though we can never be apart from it, it tends to remain eclipsed by our endless preoccupations. To enter this first stage, the seeker must have already wrested her attention away from the gravitational pull of fame, wealth, and power. There is already a clear sense that such pursuits are unlikely to bring lasting peace, meaning, joy, or wisdom. She senses or intuits the proximity of a profound unblemished something—and is determined to find it.

No Better Place

27

T he second picture, *Discovering the Footprints*, depicts a seeker at last finding the tracks of the Ox. Here there is certainty that the Ox exists and that there is in fact a legitimate path to follow. It is now a matter of walking the path which will likely require a re-prioritizing of the seeker's life. The benefit of daily sitting is becoming clear, as is the indispensability of training with a teacher and with a sangha (community of practitioners). One may also begin to engage with and appreciate other aspects of Zen practice, such as teishō; koans; kinhin (walking meditation); and working with the precepts in one's daily life.

28

In the third picture, *Catching a Glimpse of the Ox*, the seeker has a breakthrough. The result of sustained and energetic zazen, this usually occurs in the context of sesshin (an extended silent retreat). Although perhaps fleeting and shallow, it is nonetheless an incontrovertible experience of no-self-apart. As such, it may be difficult to articulate. The word *experience* feels inadequate as there is momentarily no lone self *having* an experience. But there is the sharp taste of a new freedom, of being unconfined by time, space, thoughts, and feelings. This insight is called kenshō, and while crucial to one's unfolding practice, it's not a goal or prize. Rather, it marks the beginning of a new journey based on direct personal experience instead of faith or the words of others.

29

In the fourth picture, *Catching the Ox*, the seeker has lassoed the Ox but it's a tentative hold. The mind is becoming settled but the practitioner is still often powerless in the presence of memories, thoughts, fears, and feelings. Habit-forces remain strong even though one's practice is deepening. The practitioner may believe that she's regressing but is actually just seeing the internal terrain more clearly. It's becoming obvious that practice is an increasingly subtle dropping away of self-conscious effort. Sincerity, dedication, and deep faith are required if one wishes to continue.

30

The fifth picture, *Taming the Ox*, depicts the seeker leading a partially docile Ox. This stage marks the beginning of a new way of living. Thanks to ongoing zazen and other aspects of practice, the practitioner is able, more frequently, to live intentionally, free from the habits and impulses of a hemmed-in mind. At this point there is often a growing appreciation of the Ten Grave Precepts, though not as commandments whose intent is to deny and restrict. The precepts are becoming, rather, a portrayal of a human life—your life—when liberated from the despotism of me, my, and mine. In such hours there is very naturally no killing, no stealing, no misuse of sex, no lying, no dulling the mind with drugs or alcohol, no discussion of the faults of others, no praise of oneself, no withholding of spiritual or material aid, no indulging in anger, and no defaming the Three Treasures (Buddha, Dharma, Sangha). It's not about "being good" or repressing impulses. It's simply about seeing more and more clearly how we tend to act and not act, in subtle and not-so subtle ways, that harm ourselves, the planet, and each other. And how the arising of such actions and non-actions can be consciously sidestepped. In this way the precepts function like cairns along a mountain path, revealing the way forward.

A New Zen Primer

31

The sixth picture is entitled *Riding the Ox Home*, and depicts the Oxherder playing a flute astride a docile Ox. The rope is still attached to a nose ring but it lays slack over the Ox's shoulders. Practice proceeds without effort because practice and daily life have fused. Zazen has deepened to the point where one can experience a deep rootedness regardless of surroundings or circumstances. But it's not aloofness. It's a palpable communion with that which neither arrives nor departs. Joy bubbles up more frequently and is not dependent upon things going your way. When doing zazen, zazen is doing zazen. Existential angst is increasingly replaced by a wordless intimacy with people, animals, objects, and places.

32

In the seventh picture, *The Ox is Forgotten, the Herdsman Remains*, the Ox is not visible. There is only the oxherder sitting quietly by her hut. In this stage, the awareness of peace and intimacy encountered in the sixth stage has fallen away. One can now find no self, no Ox, no realization, and no Zen. When it snows, it snows. When the snow melts, it melts. When walking, there is just walking. When laughing, there is just laughing. This is the unfathomable thusness of pure being. Here the non-practice of shikantaza naturally arises: sitting with no reflection on the sitting, no goal, no focus, no self-awareness, no privileging of one sound or sensation over another, not getting swept away by thoughts and not bothered by them when they arise. Sometimes there are thoughts and sometimes there is unmoving, delicious silence. No problem. To believe that you have attained the seventh stage is proof that you have much more zazen to do. This is because there is nothing to attain and no one apart to do the attaining. Like Newtonian physics at the center of a black hole, language does not apply here. The notion of stages is laughable. One's life is becoming more like the ceaseless, effortless movements of the ocean, each of which is just ocean: now spray, now wave, now current, now vapor, now breaking surf on barnacled rocks.

A New Zen Primer

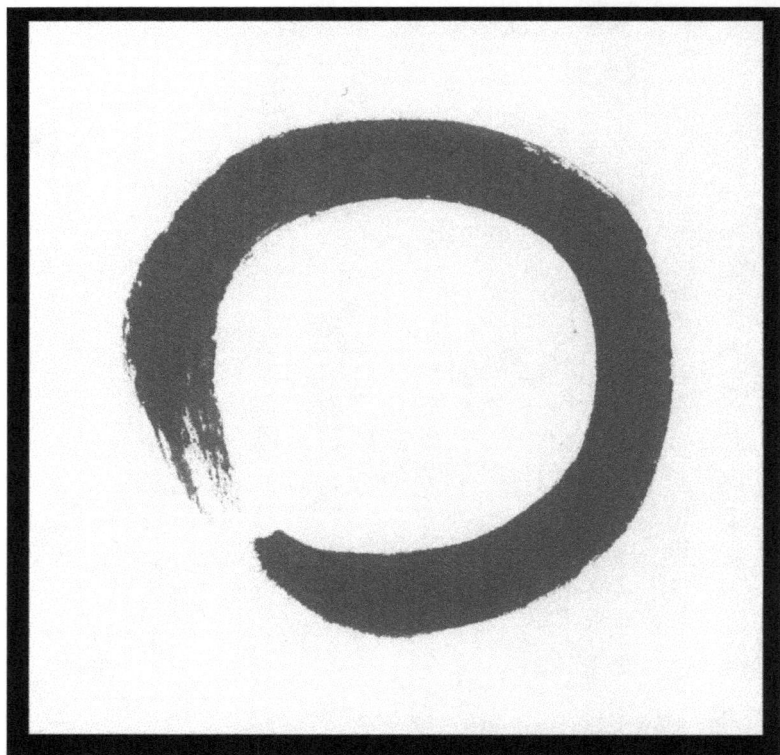

33

The eighth picture, *Both Ox and Herdsman Forgotten*, depicts an ensō, an empty circle. This is the realm of the absolute which can't be said to exist or not to exist, nor both to exist and not to exist. Of this stage, Master Sheng Yen said, "In terms of wisdom, this stage and the stage of Buddhahood are the same." To personalize what might seem unapproachable, Zen teacher Danan Henry tells the story of a dokusan encounter with his teacher Harada Tangen Roshi on the sixth night of a seven day sesshin in Obaku, Japan: "Sitting there with Roshi-sama, all preoccupations with myself disappeared. And then random and irrelevant thoughts disappeared. And then the practice disappeared, and then my self disappeared, and then the environment disappeared. There was nothing. I could not know there was nothing because there was nothing to know that there was nothing. I have no idea for how long there was nothing because there was no time. The next thing that I did know was a sound: a strange deep rumbling like a volcano beginning to erupt, a visceral primordial sound rising up out of Roshi-sama, turning into an ear-splitting shout: 'Great, perfect shikantaza!' followed by an insane rumble of wild laughter. When I left the dokusan room and walked back in the starry night to the zendo, the world was exactly the same. But I was never to be quite the same again."

A New Zen Primer

34

The ninth picture, *Returning to the Source*, depicts a tree in bloom near a running stream. The relative world of form and appearance is nothing other than the unspeakable realm of empty oneness. Form is exactly emptiness; emptiness is exactly form. They can't be teased apart because they are the same thing. At the same time, form is form and emptiness is emptiness. Logic and reason whither. You can't prove it, but it's becoming clear that the source of all existence is not separate from all existence. There is no behind-the-scenes magic kingdom from which everything arrives. The whole mysterious package is already here. This is the same world as perceived in the first oxherding picture but the mind has been deeply cleansed. As one Zen teacher put it, thinking becomes "like putting a brush to a clean sheet of paper. Every stroke comes out shining bright." This, at last, is the "peace that passeth all understanding."

35

I n the tenth picture, *Entering the Marketplace with Helping Hands*, the oxherder walks into town and interacts with other people. The search has come full circle: there has never been anything to uncover or clarify. There is no inside, no outside, and nothing apart. There is no Zen, no Tao, no enlightenment, and no ignorance. Regardless of circumstances, the oxherder's heart is at rest and her mind is at peace. She exudes no aura of saintliness and there's no concern about holy versus profane. She makes no distinction between wise and foolish people and greets presidents and homeless people in the same manner. There's no self-conscious notion of helping others or saving the planet yet she mingles easily with others to do the work that needs to be done. Her generosity, warmth, and sincerity is inspiring and contagious. She's not bound by the confines of ideology and culture yet she functions freely within them. When she cries, she cries. When she laughs, she laughs. She is comfortable in silent solitude and in conversation with strangers. If cravings, regrets, and longings arise in the mind, they quickly evaporate and she is not hobbled by them. If states of bliss arise, she is not sidetracked or seduced by them. The fundamental nature of all beings and all things possesses no characteristics and yet is vividly apparent. Anxiety about prolonging or shortening one's life falls away. While this stage represents the loftiest ideal of attainment in the tradition of Zen Buddhism, it's important to remember that "advanced" stages are not realms that only open up after decades of Herculean effort. Wherever there is authentic ongoing practice, there is the possibility of coming forth unfettered by the confines of self-concern. Even a so-called beginner can glimpse the waterfall through the leaves and be renewed, emboldened, and inspired to keep walking.

36

One of the unique aspects of Zen Buddhism is that it's both a religion and a non-religion and thus strictly neither. As a religion, it offers some clarity into the thorny perplexities of birth and death while providing steps for living a meaningful and ethically grounded life. Zen Buddhism is a non-religion in that it's nontheistic; there are no petitions to a disembodied creator and no fingers crossed for an incorporeal afterlife. Zen is also not manacled to any sacred text or institution, and is also not dependent upon belief or faith. So Zen is perhaps best cast as a practical, down-to-earth tradition that allows us to live with a radical embodiment. Like James Joyce's fictional character James Duffy, we so easily dwell "at a little distance" from our bodies. When exiled from our own life in this way, any endeavor can feel pointless because we feel like a bystander. We can even sink into a kind of nihilistic resignation where existence seems pointless. When embodied and grounded, however, the day becomes electrified. Any endeavor can be meaningful because we vanish into it and catch a glint of eternity. Religion or non-religion doesn't matter. Zen practice is a homecoming to the original body: these eyes that increasingly require glasses when reading, these naked hands, this sky, this beach, these sandpipers and scattered pieces of driftwood.

37

In order to come home we have to leave home. The Buddha took this literally and left his sleeping wife and infant son in order to practice. Fortunately, we don't have to abandon our families, a fact that the Buddha himself acknowledged later in life. What's required is much more challenging. We need to abandon the cathedral of ideology. This cathedral is where we tend to live. It's our cherished stories, both collective and private, about who we are and what the world is. This act of abandonment is the age-old mythic journey or spiritual quest. And it's not about rejecting, improving, or getting rid of mental activity. It is, rather, about not being imprisoned by mental activity. It begins with a personal resolve to see beyond our glittering rivulets of thought to "re-attain the lost union with the eternal" as Richard Tarnas put it. Such a leap can't be achieved by daily affirmations or by vowing to smile more frequently. A great effort is required. In the tradition of Zen, this great effort can be undertaken and renewed in retreats called sesshin. A sesshin provides a taste of literal homeleaving in that we do, for a brief period of time, leave behind families, careers, and daily concerns in order to devote ourselves unceasingly to practice. In a typical sesshin the practitioner engages in periods of zazen from pre-dawn darkness into the darkness of early evening, with brief periods of time for meals, dokusan (individual meetings with the teacher), chores, and rest. There is no talking (other than dokusan) and no usage of personal electronic devices. All rounds of sitting are mandatory for all participants (except in cases of personal crisis) so there's no deliberation about whether or not to sit. There is no need to know what time it is because bells wake you up each morning and bells indicate the beginning and end of all the periods of work, rest, and zazen throughout the day. There is no need to know what day it is because each day's schedule is the same. There is no need to know anything, remember anything, be anything, or do anything other than engage the practice and follow the bell-punctuated unfolding of the hours. Yastuani Roshi believed that one strong seven-day sesshin can be equivalent to practicing on one's own for two to five years.

38

B ecause all escape routes are blocked, sesshin is an opportunity to go deep. We voluntarily enter into a kind of fasting where we turn inward and learn that we can thrive without the usual preoccupations and creature comforts. The enterprise of being becomes deeper and more inclusive. But it's not a philosophy or a new worldview. It's an experience, like tasting grapefruit juice for the first time. You see that each act, each termite, each jet flying silently overhead contains and expresses the mystery. And one morning you may find that there's no place the sound of the temple bell fails to reach.

39

Sesshin can be very challenging. It's not unusual to experience dark days and dark nights of the soul where one feels utterly lost and bereft of hope. In addition, it is during sesshin when many practitioners come to appreciate Peter Matthiessen's observation that "pain in the knees is the taste of zazen." But such challenges can unlock new realms of inner resolve, fierceness, release, compassion, and strength which spill into the days and weeks following sesshin. We discover an interesting metric: the degree to which we have room for the inevitable discomforts of life is the degree to which we have room for levity and effervescence. This is another gift of zazen. We gain the superpower of being able to be with the many faces of discomfort and not run away. Discomfort is just discomfort. Stumbling is just stumbling. It doesn't mean that life sucks or that we have to re-direct the conversation or get stoned. Likewise, happiness is just happiness. We don't have to demand that it never leaves. Happiness seems to visit most reliably when we forget about being happy and instead just disappear into some simple act like walking the dog. In this way, practice becomes the art of welcoming more fully the clumsy, beautiful mess of being human. We can hold hands with all of it, even the end of the world in its sly masquerade as the end of every story and the pang of each goodbye.

40

In the poverty of sesshin, the riches of raw being are excavated. We become the unnamed character in the Robert Crumb comic strip who looks out from the page at the reader and says, "I just realized: everything is cosmic!" Time slows down and we can savor what we usually neglect or barely see. As Jim Harrison noted, "We Americans are trained to think big, talk big, act big, love big, admire bigness but then the essential mystery is in the small." If we eat our sesshin lunch outside we might gaze in silent wonder at an ant trundling the carcass of some larger dead insect across the flagstone. That's no mere ant; it's a fellow being of this solar system, no less worthy of living its life than you or I. The unrepeatability of each thing becomes poignantly apparent. A fly is the glitter of evolution; all the scientists in the world couldn't create a living biological fly from scratch. In sesshin we see, sometimes painfully so, how we take so many things for granted: spouses, neighbors, children, parents, co-workers, friends. How quick we are to judge, to dismiss, to think mostly of ourselves, or to defend the subtle trenches of private agendas. Why are we so perpetually uptight, controlling, and stressed? Why do we look out the window and sigh? Something seems to be missing. If we could only live more authentically, more generously, more from the heart. And it's not too late.

41

While the experience of time can speed up and slow down in sesshin, it can also evaporate. It's not uncommon to experience a thirty-minute round of zazen as lasting for just a moment. This is because the experience of time as duration or measurement is inextricably bound to memory (past) and imagination (future). In sesshin, memory and imagination fall away and there's just the uncanny song of each moment and each thing. We see that time only appears to pass by. It's always *now* and wherever we are is always *here*. There is no roped-off upstream or downstream to lift from the creek and reify as future or past. Reality (that which undergoes the "formality of actually occurring" to use Alfred North Whitehead's definition) only speaks in present tense. Yet it's difficult to live a fulfilling life without a sense of history and without aspirations that promise a compelling future. It is thus both useful and necessary to talk of past and future. Zen practice simply allows us to be increasingly unencumbered by the ghosts

No Better Place

of what happened and by the holograms of what we hope, believe, or fear might one day occur.

42

David Whyte suggests that instead of *homo sapiens*, human beings should be called *homo forgettens* because we so easily lose track of the simple profundity of being alive. It is indeed easy to become cynical as we grow older, to slowly become alcoholic, or to sink imperceptibly in the quicksand of a culture that seeks to turn us into dutiful media-soaked consumers. Sesshin is an opportunity to become reacquainted with a silence that pre-dates history, culture, and even geology. After the third or fourth day of sesshin, one's rate of breathing slows way down. It's not uncommon to naturally breathe just two or three breaths per minute during rounds of zazen. One becomes more aligned with primordial rhythms: the slide of shadows over the earth, a daisy opening its petals in the morning sun. We experience a unique kind of rest, deeper than sleep, that allows for the accumulation of *chi*, or *joriki* as it's called in Japanese, the fundamental life-force. The curdled chorus of those distant coyotes is not separate from my breathing. How do we manage not to appreciate the bottomlessness of each being and each thing? There is nothing inherently boring or banal. As we return to rectangular schedules and harried post-sesshin lives, the joriki slowly dissipates. But practice has deepened. Daily zazen, and daily life, is enriched. Ideally, sesshin becomes part of the ongoing cycle of practice, the endless cycle of working with others to see the mystery more clearly. Forgetting and remembering, remembering and forgetting. Who forgets? Who remembers? What are these trees, these stars, these murky dreams? Where do they come from? Why is there anything at all?

43

In addition to deepening one's zazen, sesshin deepens the gratitude one feels for sangha, the community of fellow practitioners. A powerful bond forms among people who sit together in silence hour after hour, year after year. But perhaps a bond only appears to form. Perhaps it's just the case that the unity of all things is revealed more readily among sangha. I was astonished by the deep kinship I felt with all my fellow sitters at the end of my first sesshin—even though we never spoke and even though I barely knew any of them. Zen practice is not about achieving some elevated spiritual state in isolation. It's about living a full life in a world that desperately needs connection and inclusivity. This is why regular shoulder-to-shoulder practice with others is so crucial. Zen's fulfilling quality—what Plato called *eudaimonia*—seems to have something to do with the experience of living together in harmony, even in the midst of discord. Sangha allows us to see first-hand that this is in fact possible. We see that our unburdened heart already knows the way.

44

One of the biggest challenges of Zen practice is to grasp that it has nothing to do with understanding the teachings in the way that one understands quantum mechanics or the narrative structure of *Infinite Jest*. It is, rather, about the willingness to set aside all intellection in order to confirm for yourself what the Buddha confirmed. Sutra study, scholarship, reading, and group discussion have value. Books can invigorate and inspire. But nothing very satisfying can be said or written about Zen. This is because the real journey begins where the road of language ends. As he leaves the Shire in *Lord of the Rings*, Sam Gamgee observes: "If I take one more step, it will be the furthest away from home I've ever been." Like Sam, we find that the path of Zen beckons us off-road. But it's an off-road that's always underfoot. There's no need to travel anywhere to find the Dharma unless you want to go for the pure adventure of going. This is the road that ends where it begins, the unmapped and unmappable precinct of practice *as* wisdom, suffering *as* liberation.

45

Zen practice allows us to live an ordinary life with extraordinary depth. We can take solace in the fact that people have wrestled with how to accomplish such a feat for a very long time. In Book Ten of Plato's *Republic*, written over two thousand years ago, we encounter, oddly, the character of Odysseus in a kind of bardo realm. After living his legendary life as recounted in *The Odyssey*, he is contemplating options for his next incarnation. His previous life—heroic, admired by the gods—has left him exhausted and "disenchanted with ambition." He now longs for simplicity. He finally chooses to be reborn as "a private man who has no cares." Odysseus's longing is our longing: the irrepressible hunger to get beyond that which is culturally sanctioned in order to reclaim something genuine and profound. And in the depths of zazen we encounter a conundrum-shattering profundity: there is nothing to figure out. When you make an omelet, you break the eggs and whisk them together in a bowl. That's it! Grate the cheese and crush the garlic. There's nothing missing! The entire cosmos is your sous chef. Such intimacy *is* living a life with no cares, whether making an omelet or protesting a war. But this simplicity and freedom are accessible only if we're willing and able to forfeit our master narratives about how things should be. Only then can we see what's right in front of us: the miraculous as the ordinary, the ordinary as the miraculous.

46

Zen practice is much more than just doing zazen. One of the sharpest tools in the Zen training kit is the koan. Usually taken up as brief passages of text, koans appear paradoxical because they point to and reveal that which outstrips all reckoning. As such, they can't be cracked open by the rational mind. One famous koan goes like this: *The ten thousand things return to the one. Where does the one return to?* In working with any koan, we sit with it in zazen, silently reciting it—breathing it—over and over until there's no gap between us and the koan. And during dokusan we demonstrate our understanding to the teacher. In the case of this particular koan, if you say "the one returns to the ten thousand things" you miss the point. If you bow, remain silent, or just do zazen, you also miss it. A koan invites us to see and embody its particular vantage point of the ineffable, to step forth and participate in the playful tension between verbal and nonverbal, form and emptiness, self and other.

47

A koan is a sculpture made of words that reveals the fiction of me, my, and mine, and thus the groundlessness of greed, anger, and delusion. All we have to do is disappear into the landscape of each koan. In doing so, we free ourselves from the bog of identity narratives. It's like regaining a superpower from childhood where we're able to shapeshift into a horse, a dragon, or a unicorn and then switch back to being Soren, Anders, or Mirabelle. In working with koan after koan we move again and again between self and no-self, gaining a clearer understanding of how they co-arise. Like north and south, one infers and includes the other. And when we see the shared root of this symbiosis, we venture beyond self and no-self entirely, here and now, in the astonishing act of cleaning out the stinking cat box.

48

To fail to grasp the heart of a koan is in fact a way of circling closer and eventually seeing it. "Ever tried. Ever failed. No matter. Try Again. Fail again. Fail better," says Samuel Beckett, and this approach to failure is instructive. When you fail to stay with the breath or with the koan, and find yourself daydreaming, just notice the drifting and without judgment return to the breath or to the koan. Failure here is thus not failure. It's simply the living terrain of practice. Drifting away, noticing the drifting, and returning to your practice *is* precisely the path.

49

By revealing the limitations of linear, sequential thinking, koans thwart our intellectual cunning. We see that daily life outstrips our ability to know it. As Albert Einstein put it, "As far as laws of mathematics refer to reality, they are not certain; and as far as they are certain, they do not refer to reality." As a result of each koan's unique power to show that we can't figure out reality—that greatest of all whodunits—our humility deepens. Each of us is making it up as we go, swimming in eternity as eternity. And each of us is a once-born and a soon-to-die, like the rising sun this morning that improvised a little jazz number with the clouds.

50

Koans nudge us over the cliff of birth and death into a keen and generous silence. *From where you are, stop the sound of that distant bell.* To grasp this koan is to grasp the sound of a bell that has nothing to do with distance and nothing to do with lack of distance. It is the sound of a bell which has nothing to do with sound and nothing to do with lack of sound.

51

In working with koans, contradiction yields to complementarity. Birth and death cease to be bickering opposites and begin to reclaim their common ground. A fun koan about birth and death is: *Where does a flame go when it's extinguished?* Where do you and I go when we're extinguished? The present moment is unceasingly dying and being reborn, so much so that there is no present moment. The death of each exhalation is the birth of each inhalation. There is no beginning and no end. To quote Einstein again, "Energy cannot be created or destroyed, it can only be changed from one form to another." The restless anguish of being human stems from a deeply ingrained resistance to the fact that everything is in a constant state of transformation. Nothing is ownable, definable, or pin-downable. And this is good news because the fundamental nature of all things, including you, me, and the flame of a candle, is free. But koan work is not about explaining, agreeing, understanding, or fine tuning a view. Where *does* a flame go when it's extinguished?

52

It can be tempting to believe that zazen itself has some kind of net-positive influence in the world. And it may. But trickle-down Dharma is not enough. Our zazen needs to walk out of the zendo and engage the koan of everyday life: driving the Zamboni; bringing the dying dog to the vet; raising children; raising political hell; meeting the ongoing challenges of an intimate relationship. So there are practices which function as zazen off the cushion. Kinhin (walking meditation) is such a practice. When doing kinhin, the hands are positioned at the navel, the open left hand gently holding the right fist. While kinhin may be a break from seated zazen, it's not a break from practice. The breath is keyed to the slow, deliberate movements of walking. When the mind wanders, notice the wandering and rejoin the breath, the swaying of the body, the soft rustle of clothing, the gentle flip of the heels of the person in front of you, the cold floor, the transfer of weight along the sole of the foot. You find that you can enter this ordinary act as though stepping into an old stupa on some remote mountain pass in Tibet. The tired internal babbling drops away and it's the smell of incense that walks around the zendo.

53

Ceremony and liturgy can also help expand the geographical range of our practice. Circum-ambulating in the low light of the zendo, hands palm-to-palm in gasshō, candles burning on the altar, the gentle waft of incense, chanting the *Kannon Sutra of Timeless Life*:

> *Kanzeon*
> *Praise to Buddha*
> *All are one with Buddha*
> *All awake to Buddha*
> *Buddha, Dharma, Sangha*
> *Our True-nature is eternal, joyous, selfless, and pure*
> *Through the day Kanzeon*
> *Through the night Kanzeon*
> *Thought after thought arises in mind*
> *Thought after thought is not separate from mind*
> *Each moment itself is mind*

we have the chance to step free from the coffin of what year it is, what country we're from, how old we are, who our enemies are, what our gender is, why we're pissed off at our parents. In this flirtation with the timeless, sangha brothers and sisters are fellow pilgrims with whom we've walked this path for eons. A kind of inner sanctum is revealed but it manifests as just this ordinary place and just this ordinary moment. If we embrace the act of liturgy or ceremony fully enough, it's not merely a transitional practice. It's the living Dharma itself: the news that stays news.

54

There is no such thing as a Zen state of mind. There is only the possibility of being intimate with your surroundings and with your situation. At such a time there is no Zen, no Buddha, no enlightenment, no ignorance, no saving the world, and no one to save it. This is how you save the world.

55

To practice Zen is to forget about Zen. But this is not to say that practice is unnecessary or that it should eventually be abandoned. Without practice there's something out there called Zen. Without practice there's something out there called Dharma. Without practice there is someone out there called Buddha.

56

There is no need to malign ego, that most convincing and persistent notion of a me apart. Ego has no color, no odor, no form, no mass, and no taste. What is there to malign? It's just that this non-existent phantom somehow keeps us under house arrest. But so what? The more we practice, the less seriously we take our weird hauntings, obsessions, self-loathings, and self-promotions. Let them come. We don't have to run from them, indulge them, or act out. They're just patterns of clouds. We gain a deeper acceptance and sense of humor about the ubiquity of human vanities, faults, and failings. There's no need to hide our shortcomings and personality flaws or to pretend to be someone we're not. This is because fundamentally there are no shortcomings or faults. All our burdensome character armor falls away when we realize that there's nothing to defend and no one to defend it. Paraphrasing David Whyte, "Spiritual practice is not about becoming perfect; it's about recovering an inner completeness which grants us the freedom to limp fully and without reservation."

57

When the machinery of self-apart stops even momentarily, we stand beyond realization and ignorance, beyond big mind and small mind, beyond Nirvana and Samsara, beyond birth and beyond death. This may sound hopelessly twee. But what happens when ideas, fears, theories, and ideologies actually do drop away? What happens when the great silence joins you in the kitchen asking for nothing in return? Is brewing a cup of tea enlightened or ignorant? Is it an act of big mind or small mind? In the bare act of sipping tea, who are you?

58

There is a slow Copernican shift, in terms of how we see our life and this world, that unfolds with sustained practice. The path becomes less about an atomized self seeking spiritual truth and more about facing and actualizing a natural inclusion and wholeness. Practice becomes less and less self-conscious. As though emerging from solitary confinement, we become reconstituted. There's no question any more of belonging or not belonging. The Big Dipper is still inconceivably far away but it's also somehow as close as our heartbeat. The deepest questions about life and death feel like cherished friends. The dreaded metaphysical abyss is more like a feather bed. We acquire immunity to the need for intellectual closure. There's less need to compare, judge, and categorize. The hidden motives and agendas of those around us become less interesting. It's easier to listen. It's easier to give, to laugh, to cry. Our operating system is not ego or Microsoft or Apple. Increasingly, it is the fathomless Tao.

59

Because of the seamless nature of things, any act we perform is *de facto* an act of the earth. This means that when you do zazen, the earth does zazen. The small contains the large; the large is precisely the small. The earth is not out there. So we can do zazen *and* we can serve others. And these two poles of engagement eventually cease to be so different. From a Zen Buddhist perspective this means that it's impossible to save your own ass without saving the asses of others and it's impossible to save the asses of others without saving your own ass. Kukai, the 9th century Japanese poet, saw it this way:

> *The hand moves*
> *and the fire's whirling*
> *takes different shapes*
> *—all things change when we do*

60

In most Zen Buddhist centers and temples, the Bodhisattva Vows, or Great Vows for All, are chanted once a day:

> *The many beings are countless;*
> *I vow to save them.*
> *Greed, hatred, and ignorance rise endlessly;*
> *I vow to abandon them.*
> *Dharma gates are countless;*
> *I vow to wake to them.*
> *Buddha's way is unsurpassed;*
> *I vow to embody it fully.*

Each vow is unattainable (and perhaps even audacious-sounding) but I *vow* to attain each one. To vow to attain the unattainable is to understand that there is no end to the path. There are no edges or boundaries. The greed, hatred, and ignorance of a multi-national corporation dumping toxic waste into a lake is my own greed, hatred, and ignorance. It's just a different context and a different scale. The wisdom and compassion of the Buddha is my own wisdom and compassion. It's just that these qualities tend to hide in the back yard without engaged practice. We have a choice. What kind of field am I cultivating in the minutes and hours that I walk the earth? For whose benefit am I living this one precious life?

61

The Old Testament story of the Fall of Man can be read as a metaphor for humanity's tumble from animal nakedness into civilization. Slowly, somehow, nature/Eden became something separate, something over there to subdue, control, partition off, and dominate. As a result of this rift, we humans tend to feel unmoored, incomplete, and lacking. This is our peculiar restlessness, a collective, globe-girdling itch that we can't quite scratch. And the plundered, imperiled world as we know it is the result. Maybe the Singularity will save us: the moment in the not-too-distant future when computer code and genetic code will fuse and we will engineer ourselves into something trans-human. But there is a more elemental singularity which is already here. It's just well-disguised. It's the fact that we never fell from nature in the first place. There is nothing but nature. There is nothing but cosmos. Human beings secrete technology the same way bees secrete honey. There is nothing artificial about artificial intelligence; it's just a highly sophisticated hand axe fashioned by language-mad primates. Of course, the big question remains: in our rapacious pursuit of some state of ultimate fulfillment, can we halt or reverse the cascade of noxious processes that our species has set in motion? How? A good first step might be to wake up to the river-roar of wholeness that each one of us is.

62

If reason is an ornithologist, Zen is a raven. But it's not solely an either/or proposition. We can engage the world rationally *and* we can relearn how to inhabit and navigate this animal body-mind with its untold, untellable, earthbound mysteries.

63

From one perspective, zazen is a method. But ultimately it does not bird-dog toward some higher or better state of mind. This is because zazen *is* mind, the original mind of who you are, neither begotten nor unbegotten—the mind that slips the net of birth and death while dying and being born.

64

This unique and subtle path is not about looking on the bright side or seeing the cup as half full. It's about freeing ourselves from an interior maze of unrest by realizing that we're already free. It's about moving beyond abstraction to experience and actualize, more and more deeply, the undivided nature we share with all beings and all things. It's about giving these needling habits of mind permission to look up from their work. To what end? To come to know our inherent joy, compassion, and wisdom. To live this brief life with authenticity, generosity, gratitude, and depth—for our own benefit and for the benefit of others. To see that we don't have to wander in a dunescape of recycled obsessions and yearnings. Life is fleeting. The affairs of the world will never be settled. Where are you going?

APPENDIX | Sample Sesshin (Retreat) Schedule
(varies among lineages)

4:50AM	wake up
5:15	tea ceremony, encouraging words from the teacher
5:30	rounds of zazen with kinhin (walking meditation)
7:00	breakfast
7:30	work/rest period
9:00	chanting service
9:35	rounds of zazen with kinhin & dokusan (private interviews with teacher)
12:00PM	lunch
12:30	work/rest period
2:00	zazen
2:30	teisho (Dharma talk by the teacher)
3:30	periods of zazen with kinhin & dokusan
5:00	yoga
5:30	recitations

5:45	supper
6:15	work/rest period
7:00	tea ceremony
7:10	periods of zazen with kinhin & dokusan
9:00	evening ritual
9:15	yaza (informal, optional zazen)
9:15	tea and crackers

NOTES

chapter 1

the ground of being
Paul Tillich, *Systemic Theology, Volume 1*
(University of Chicago Press, 1973)

universal being
Shunryu Suzuki, *Zen Mind, Beginner's Mind*
(Weatherhill, 1970)

the which than which there is no whicher
Alan Watts, *Myth and Ritual in Christianity*
(Beacon Press, 1971)

chapter 4

an imprisonment so total that the prisoner doesn't even know he's locked up
David Foster Wallace, Kenyon College
commencement address, 2005

there are no strangers
Thomas Merton, *I Have Seen What I was Looking For* (New City Press, 2005)

chapter 5

the same last name
John Tarrant, *The Light Inside the Dark* (Harper Perennial, 1999)

chapter 7

discipline of seated stillness...discovered as far back as the Upper Paleolithic
adapted from a suggestion by Gary Snyder in *The Real Work: Interviews & Talks 1964-1979* (New Directions, 1980)

chapter 9

Zen practice tends to become a hobby, made to fit the needs of the ego.
Robert Aitken, *The Mind of Clover: Essays in Zen Buddhist Ethics* (North Point Press, 1982)

chapter 10

The solution to the problem of life is seen in the vanishing of this problem.
Ludwig Wittgenstein; Bertrand Russell (intro.), *Tractatus Logico-Philosophicus* (Kegan Paul, Trench, Trubner and Co, 1922)

chapter 11

...infinity in the palm of your hand / And eternity in an hour.
William Blake, "Auguries of Innocence," 1803

chapter 12

All the way to heaven is heaven
St. Catherine of Siena, *The Letters of Saint Catherine of Siena* (ACMRS Publications, 2000)

chapter 14

Even if all possible scientific questions be answered, the problems of life have still not been touched at all.
Ludwig Wittgenstein; Bertrand Russell (intro.), *Tractatus Logico-Philosophicus* (Kegan Paul, Trench, Trubner and Co, 1922)

chapter 15

the narrow chambers of the brain
Antonin Artaud, *The Theater and Its Double* (Grove Press, 1958)

WHY! who makes much of a miracle? / As to me, I know of nothing else but miracles
Walt Whitman, "Miracles," first published in *Leaves of Grass* (Fowler & Wells, 1856) as "Poem of Perfect Miracles."

chapter 19

never divides itself into self and other, or subject and object, but merely wears the face of self and other.
Keizan Jokin, *The Record of Transmitting the Light,* (Wisdom Publications, 2003)

chapter 20

If you see me suffering, that's OK. That's just suffering Buddha.
A story that circulates in Zen circles: original source, if in writing, unknown.

chapter 21

And the day came when the risk to remain tight in a bud was more painful than the risk it took to blossom.
Frequently attributed to Anaïs Nin but the original source is unknown.

chapter 37

re-attain the lost union with the eternal
Richard Tarnas, *The Passion of the Western Mind* (Ballantine Books, 1993)

chapter 39

pain in the knees is the taste of zazen
Peter Matthiessen quoting Yamada Roshi,
"Emptying the Bell: an Interview with Peter
Matthiessen," *Tricycle*, Fall 1993

chapter 40

**We Americans are trained to think big,
talk big, act big, love big, admire bigness
but then the essential mystery is in the
small.**
Jim Harrison, *Off to the Side: a Memoir*
(Grove Press, 2002)

chapter 41

the formality of actually occurring
frequently attributed to Alfred North
Whitehead by Terence McKenna: original
source unknown

chapter 42

homo forgettens
David Whyte, *Crossing the Unknown Sea:
Work as a Pilgrimage of Identity* (Riverhead
Books, 2002)

chapter 48

Ever tried. Ever failed. No matter. Try Again. Fail again. Fail better.
Samuel Beckett, *Worstward Ho* (Grove Press, 1984)

chapter 56

Spiritual practice...fully and without reservation.
Adapted from a performance/talk by David Whyte in Boulder in the 1990s

Acknowledgements

Thank you to the following people who provided crucial support, in different ways at different times, as I wrote this book: James Churches; Matthew Cooperman; Danan Henry Roshi; Jeffrey Duvall; Tim Gale; Jiun Hosen, Osho; Francis Kaklauskas; David Martin; Rafe Martin; Elizabeth Olson; Mike Parker; Gillian Parrish; Andrew Schelling; Peggy Metta Sheehan; Leda Swann; and the Old Bones Sangha.

About the Author

Hoag Holmgren is an apprentice teacher in the Harada-Yasutani lineage of Zen Buddhism. A poet and educator as well, he is author of the poetry collection *paleos* (Middle Creek, 2019) and co-author of *Meaningful Grading: A Guide for Faculty in the Arts* (West Virginia University Press, 2019). His poetry, fiction, and nonfiction have appeared in numerous literary journals and venues. He lives with his family in Nederland, CO.

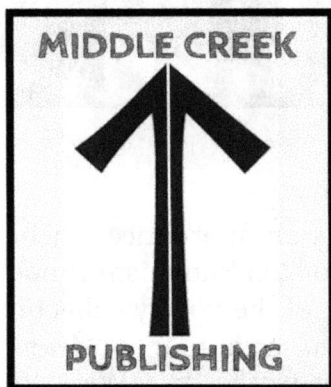

Middle Creek Publishing Titles

ABOUT MIDDLE CREEK PUBLISHING

MIDDLE CREEK PUBLISHING believes that responding to the world through art & literature — and sharing that response — is a vital part of being an artist.

MIDDLE CREEK PUBLISHING is a company seeking to make the world a better place through both the means and ends of publishing. We are publishers of quality literature in any genre from authors and artists, both seasoned and as-yet undervalued, with a great interest in works which may be considered to be, illuminate or embody any aspect of contemplative Human Ecology, defined as the relationship between humans and their natural, social, and built environments.

MIDDLE CREEK's particular interest in Human Ecology, is meant to clarify an aspect of the quality in the works we will consider for publication, and is meant as a guide to those considering submitting work to us. Our interest is in publishing works illuminating the Human experience through words, story or other content that connects us to each other, our environment, our history and our potential deeply and more consciously.

MIDDLE CREEK PUBLISHING
9027 Cascade Avenue
Beulah, CO 81023 USA

Founding Editor: David Anthony Martin
Editor@MiddleCreekPublishing.com

Website: www.middlecreekpublishing.com

AFIELD | Journal of Human Ecology:
https://mcpafieldjournal.com/

NOTES

NOTES

NOTES

www.ingramcontent.com/pod-product-compliance
Lightning Source LLC
Chambersburg PA
CBHW070332090426
42733CB00012B/2453